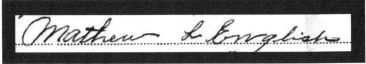

1st Sergeant 149th Co., Coast Artillery Corps,

Fort Casey, Washington

Captain, 344th Battalion, Tank Corps, A.E.F.

A Hero for All Time

A Hero for All Time

A Decorated Soldier
of World War I,

Math L. English

from
Fort Casey, Washington

Anita Burdette-Dragoo
With Foreword by Steven J. Kobylk

Front Cover: Math L. English, wearing a mix of on- and off-duty apparel, hunting wild game on Whidbey Island near Fort Casey. *Math English personal artifacts, Fort Casey Collection.*

Back Cover: Distinguished Service Cross and Oak Leaf Cluster awarded to Math L. English on March 28, 1925. *Photo Credit: Courtesy of Steven J. Kobylk.*

Frontispiece: Math L. English in his Coast Artillery undress uniform wearing his Marksman A badge. *Math English personal artifacts, Fort Casey Collection.*

Published in the United States of America

To the men and women of the American Armed Forces

Who have served their nation faithfully and honorably,

Doing their soldierly duty

Silently, without seeking acclaim or glory.

Table of Contents

Foreword

On the left side of the lawn in front of the Island County Court House in Coupeville, Washington stands a memorial to those who died serving their country during WWI. The "Died in Service" memorial is just like thousands of other memorials still standing throughout the country honoring our fallen heroes. Over time and the changing of generations, the history and stories of the individuals' names engraved on the memorials can become vague or lost, but their sacrifice remains fresh for future generations. In the case of the Island County memorial, seven of the eight names engraved were local men who lived most or all of their lives in the county and have a rich heritage with many families that still live in the area—names from well-established places by 1918: Bayview, Langley, Camano, San de Fuca, Maxwelton, Smith's Prairie, and Crescent Harbor. However there is one name that at first glance seems completely out of place and puzzling. His name is Math L. English from Fort Casey. Being "from" the relatively new Fort Casey implies that Math L. English was a career soldier, not originally from the area and without deep roots in Island County.

This begs the questions, who is Math L. English? Where was he born and raised? Why did he consider Fort Casey home instead of the town where he was born and raised? What circumstances took him from the relative safety of Island County to the battlefields of

Europe? And finally, what relationship and adventures did he have with a General who thought so highly of Math L. English that he wrote a poem about him? A poem of such significance that it was read at the General's own funeral 27 years after the death of Math L. English?

This book addresses these questions and more. Anita Dragoo has spent countless hours of research on the topic and presents a fascinating picture of Math L. English and the events/relationships surrounding his life. While understandably several technical aspects of his service in the Coast Artillery have been simplified for the book's audience, selected life events at Fort Casey are well represented.

I hope you enjoy reading the book as much as I have reviewing the Coast Artillery related sections.

Steven J. Kobylk
-Coast Defense Study Group
(www.cdsg.org)
Whidbey Field Representative
-Board Member, Coast Artillery
Museum, Ft. Worden, WA.
January 2016

Author's Notes and Acknowledgements

Sometime after an heir of Math English, Mrs. Muriel Smith of Victoria, British Columbia, donated his Army footlocker containing his military memorabilia to Fort Casey State Park in western Washington in 2004, I was given the opportunity, as a park docent, to "search for the human interest" among its contents. The poem written by General Patton especially intrigued me and seemed to be a good starting point. My task, I determined, was to discover "the path" set by Captain English from Gibson, Georgia, the town which his obituary identified as his birthplace, through Fort Casey, a Coast Artillery fortification near Coupeville, Washington, intersecting with the Tank Corps commanded by General Patton, and ending in an American cemetery in northeastern France. I decided to work from both the beginning and the end and hoped to join them together at the Distinguished Service Cross and Oak Leaf cluster which English had been awarded.

Many people deserve my thanks for the help they provided. First and foremost, I thank Steven Kobylk, Whidbey Field Representative of the Coast Defense Study Group and board member of the Coast Artillery Museum at Fort Worden, Washington, who carefully photographed and documented each item in Captain

English's footlocker when it was donated to Fort Casey. Steven's knowledge and help was invaluable in decoding the significance of the medals, badges, and pins, and I depended on his explanations of the photos and the early history and workings of Fort Casey and the Coast Artillery Corps. My greatest thrill occurred the day Steven opened Captain English's footlocker and let me examine, hands on, the letters, the medals, even the gas mask and military cap once worn by Captain English.

My sincere thanks goes also to Gloria Wahlin, the Washington State University Admiralty Head Lighthouse Coordinator who handed me the binder of photographs that Steven Kobylk had taken and urged me to search for more of the story. We agreed that the handsome man shown in the photos and described in the letters conveyed a sense of decency and honor which deserved to be told.

Thank you, also, to the people of Coupeville, especially Roger Sherman, for preserving the history of their community and nearby Fort Casey. Sarah Aldrich, archivist for the Island County Historical Society at the Janet Enzmann Library and Archives in Coupeville spent one morning searching with me through their collection of photographs and newspapers for Math English. Library assistants at the Sno-Isle Library Oak Harbor Branch taught me how to search their microfilm of *The Island County Times* dated from 1909-1918.

Matt Swint, history teacher at Glascock County High School in Gibson, Georgia sent me information about the demographics and history of the rural community where Math was born and grew up.

Ernie Peischel, Math's grand-nephew, provided family genealogy information.

John Fields and Jeff Brashares of the *Buick Heritage Alliance* helped identify the model and date of the Buick in Math's photo.

Judy Savage, a personal friend, explained the significance of Math's involvement in the Nile Temple Nobles of the Mystic Shrine in Seattle and the activities in which he might have participated.

Barbara Taylor, Museum Exhibits Specialist at the Fort George G. Meade Museum, Fort Meade, Maryland, introduced me to Patrick Osborn, a local historian there, who identified World War I photos and recommended Dale Wilson's excellent book on the early Tanks Corps, *Treat 'Em Rough*. Wilson's detailed research enabled me to recreate Math's activities once he arrived in France and follow Math's movements nearly day by day into battle.

Thank you to the family of Lieutenant Harvey Harris for publishing his letters from France during the war. What a poignant discovery to read about Captain English's last night on earth!

Let me also acknowledge the power of the Internet which enabled me to virtually visit Fort Screvens, Georgia and Fort Adams, Rhode Island, Coast Artillery forts where Math served. Via Internet I could view the cemetery in France where Math is buried as well as see his grandfather's grave in Georgia. Google satellite photos substituted for actual visits to the Meuse-Argonne region and the village of Cheppy, France where English earned his first Distinguished Service Cross.

My entire search has been a wonderful adventure. Most important is the feeling that I have made the acquaintance of a sincere and dedicated American patriot, a man who inspired his associates, who made them his friends, and who led them to serve America as he did, with honor.

A Hero for All Time

~~~

**A Decorated Soldier
of World War I,**

Math L. English

**from
Fort Casey, Washington**

Prologue

Through the gray morning mist, thickened with acrid smoke from heavy artillery bombardment, faint silhouettes of American infantrymen bounded out of deep earthen trenches, running across No-Man's-Land toward enemy lines. An incessant reverberation followed mortar shells that soared through the air and struck the ground with thuds, sending geysers of mud, grass, and rocks skyward. The rat-ta-tat-tat of machine guns competed with the rumble of tanks, drowning out voices that shouted orders. The date was September 26, 1918. In this, the "War to End All Wars," Allied soldiers were launching their largest offensive yet against German forces in the Argonne Forest along the Meuse River in northeastern France.

As the sun rose higher, the fog lifted and swirled away, revealing two officers standing together on the parapet of a trench. Below them, a heavy tank, bogged down within the narrow ditch, blocked the route of four more tanks lined up behind it. For over fifteen minutes, under continual machine gun fire, a cluster of infantrymen surrounded the mired tank, tossing away shovelsful of dirt from its tracks until, at last, the massive weapon began to roll ahead. One of the supervising officers atop the trench stepped out, leading the driver forward, calmly oblivious to the bullets whizzing past him, pinging and bouncing off the tank's steel sides.

Captain Math L. English, guiding his company of tanks on foot into combat, would be awarded the Distinguished Service Cross for his valor on that morning. The other soldier on the parapet, Colonel George S. Patton, Jr., would be wounded later that day and spend the rest of the war recuperating behind the lines. After the guns of World War I at last fell silent and the Armistice was signed on November 11, 1918, that courageous image of Captain English under fire remained vivid in Patton's mind, and its inspiration would endure until Patton's death twenty-seven years later.[1]

Both Math English and George Patton, Jr. belonged to a generation that believed in honor and sacrifice—that patriots had a duty to uphold and defend the principles on which America was founded. Nearly a century has passed since America entered that first war of the 20th century, and four more generations have worn its uniform in combat. Before the details fade completely into the mists of time, let us travel the path of the Fort Casey Coast Artillery soldier whose heroism in France deeply affected the life of one of the second war's most famous generals and set an example for American soldiers ever since.

The Captain and the Colonel

When Captain English and Colonel Patton first met in early 1918, each had served nearly a decade or more in the United States Army, but neither was a seasoned combat veteran. English was the older of the two, born November 8, 1881, four years and three days before Patton's birth on November 11. They may have noticed that not only did they nearly share the same birthday, but both had married in 1910 and become fathers the following year.

Their life journeys, which converged in Bourg, France at America's first Tanks Corps training center, however, bore little resemblance. Patton's academy training prepared him for leadership roles. English, on the other hand, rose through the ranks of the enlisted, and he only received his commission after America entered the war in 1917.

Patton's life is well-documented and available elsewhere. Most of what is known about English's early life is derived from the military memorabilia contained in the Army footlocker that his heirs donated to Fort Casey State Park, Washington in 2004.

Math's grandfather, Joel Isaac English, and his wife, Rebecca, had nine children, four girls and five boys.[2] Their seventh, Matthew Lewis, was still in his twenties when he died one month before the birth of his namesake and only son. Because several other family members also bore the name Matthew, the son adopted the nickname of Math at some undetermined time and used it officially during his military career. According to family lore, Math's mother, Susan, died early in his life as well. Although his grandparents lived until 1890 and 1896, Math was raised by his aunt, Nancy English Logue, and her husband, William Rooks Logue. Their daughter, Sallie Rebecca, was born when Math was ten years old.

Math spent his early life in the small farming village of Gibson, Georgia, east of Atlanta, where yeoman farmers grew row crops on 100 acres or less—wheat, rye, soybeans, corn, and cotton— and members of the English family operated a grain mill in the community. By contrast, Georgie Patton's maternal grandfather held vast citrus orchards and vineyards near San Gabriel, California, and his father was a prominent attorney and politician. He grew up in an affluent lifestyle that Math would never experience.

The two men may not have discovered their shared Confederate background. Records in Georgia show that Math's uncle, William Logue, enlisted in the Confederate Army on September 3, 1861 at Camp McDonald as a private in Company A of the 22nd Regiment, Georgia Infantry, and mustered out of Company B as a sergeant.[3] One can imagine that young Math learned about the Civil War by listening to Confederate veterans, including his uncle, spinning their war stories. Perhaps he idolized the old heroes dressed in frayed grey uniforms and caps marching with honor in village parades and dreamed of becoming a soldier himself. But the exploits of the Logue Confederates probably did not match the ones told to Georgie about his grandfather, George Smith Patton, and seven of his great-uncles who were Virginian officers during the Civil War. Throughout his life, Georgie Patton felt compelled to equal if not surpass the valorous reputations of his Uncle Tazewell and Grandfather Patton who both were mortally wounded.

The early education of the two boys differed vastly. Georgie Patton benefited from his privileged family circumstances. Even though he suffered from dyslexia, his aunt tutored him at home by reading to him for three to four hours every day until he was twelve years old. His father also read to him—military history—and filled his mind with the family tales of the Civil War. Georgie would attend the Virginia Military Institute (VMI) for a year before his father managed an appointment for him to West Point, the Army's academy from which he would graduate five years later.

Math, on the other hand, apparently did not even attend high school for there was none in Gibson nor in all of Glascock County, Georgia during his teen years, yet he learned to read and write sufficiently well to be accepted into the Coast Artillery with its rigid standards of literacy and physical fitness. Most of the young men in the region grew up working as a farm hands with little expectation of leaving Gibson. But shortly after reaching the age of majority, Math left home to join the Regular Army near Savannah. Very possibly, in the mind of a youth with few local options, Army life offered the promise of action and glory as well as room and board and a regular, though meager, income.

Math English and the Coast Artillery Corps

Two decades before Math English was born, American military technology changed in significant ways that would affect his life. The battle during the Civil War between the ironclad ships *Monitor* and *Merrimack* had signaled a change in the Navy's role from defensive to offensive while the additional development of rifled cannons with a longer range rendered muzzle-loading cannons obsolete and left the old stone and mason forts along America's coasts vulnerable to attack. The United States Navy began a modernization program in 1883 as Math English was growing up in rural Georgia, for American military defenses and technology were in need of significant upgrading.

A review board appointed by President Grover Cleveland and directed by Secretary of War William C. Endicott recommended in 1886 that strategic harbors in 29 locations should be fortified by earthen and concrete batteries with underground magazines which blended in with their surroundings. These should be dispersed over large areas and equipped with breech-loading guns, mortars of various sizes, and rifled guns on disappearing carriages. Also, the adjoining waters should be planted with electrically-controlled mine fields.   In 1888, funds were allocated to develop the arms and equipment and to establish an ordnance board, but then as now, Congress moved slowly with fortification appropriations. More than a decade passed before construction began on the forts that would figure in Math English's career.[4]

The complexities and diversities of modernized field artillery and coast artillery further led to the reorganization of the Artillery Corps in 1907, dividing it into Field Artillery Companies and Coast Artillery Companies (CAC). Individual units within the CAC were authorized up to 109 enlisted men while officers were primarily selected from West Point graduates.

Among the memorabilia that Math's family donated to Fort Casey is a *First Class Gunner* medal indicating that Math was attached to the 5th Company (Mortars) Coast Artillery which was stationed from 1901 to 1909 at Fort Screvens, Georgia. Promotions to First Class were awarded to second-class gunners who passed both a written and a practical exam with a score of 90% or better, and the crossed cannon *First Class Gunner* medal in Math's possession was awarded to those in the top 25% of the qualification group. Apparently soon after Math turned 21 on November 8, 1902, he traveled the 125 miles or so from Gibson to Fort Screvens to enlist. Not only was it close to his home, but some considered the coast artillery as being more of a choice assignment. Construction of the new fort on Tybee Island near the mouth of the Savannah River had begun in 1897 and consisted of six batteries for heavy artillery including Battery Habersham with eight 12-inch mortars. One would expect newly-formed units to work with modern equipment, live in newer, more comfortable garrisons, and afford more openings for career advancement.

We may never learn why or exactly when Math transferred from Fort Screvens to the west coast forts of Flagler and Casey. He may have been sent to fill the new billets as the Coast Artillery expanded or he may have traveled at his own request. After all, he was young, single, without parents or siblings to tie him to home. Why not seize the opportunity for adventure? Other choices he made later in life indicate a predilection for innovation and risk-taking.

Fortifying the entrance to Puget Sound was not a high priority when the Endicott Report was completed in 1886 because, frankly, the Puget Sound region was considered too sparsely developed. That attitude began changing as Washington became a state on November 11, 1889, the Navy established a shipyard near Bremerton in 1891, the Northern Pacific Railroad reached Seattle in 1893, and gold was discovered in Alaska in 1896. Memories of the infamous Pig War and its ultimate resolution with the 1871 Treaty of Washington, including the arbitration of border issues by Kaiser Wilhelm I of Germany, were still fresh enough that when the British Naval Forces built a base at Victoria on Vancouver Island, they raised American concern that Canada might attempt to retake the San Juan Islands.

By 1896, government plans called for construction of several new fortifications throughout the region. Fort Casey at Admiralty Head, Fort Worden near Port Townsend, and Fort Flagler on Marrowstone Point would protect the narrow inlet into Puget Sound while Fort Ward would guard the entrance to Port Orchard and the naval shipyard. A fifth, Fort Whitman, would guard Deception Pass at the north end of Whidbey Island. Civilian workers under the Corps of Engineers began that year preparing the ground for concrete batteries to support the guns, the 12-inch mortars, and the mine field. The conflict between Spain and America which erupted into warfare in April 1898 intensified the urgency to complete the work and protect Northwest shipping although there was no real threat that the Spanish fleet would attack.

The CAC collar insignia of crossed cannons above the number 26 found among the devices in Math's footlocker would indicate that he reported first to the 26th Company mortar battery based at Fort Flagler on Marrowstone Point during that time.

In 1904, Fort Casey's Commanding Officer requested that Math be transferred across the channel to Admiralty Head under orders to join the 63rd company which operated the mortar batteries Schenck and Seymour and promoted him to the rank of sergeant. The 63rd became the 149th company in 1908. A photo of the 149th in dress blues with rifles shows Sergeant English wearing a Gun Commander's patch. As such, he would have been a non-commissioned officer responsible for the training of the soldiers assigned to him, supervising their maintenance of the mortars and inspecting each mortar before it was fired.

First Sgt. English, far left with back to camera, 149th Company, evening colors formation in full dress M1902 uniforms, in front of Company Barracks #17, Fort Casey, Washington. *Math English personal artifacts: Fort Casey Collection.*

When Math was promoted to First Sergeant in 1915, as the highest ranking Non-Commissioned Officer (NCO) in the 149th Company, he would have had supervisory duties and answered directly to the company commander. Each day, he would have taken roll call at reveille, noted soldiers on sick call, and made the morning report. Other duties involved inspecting the guard detail and marching them for ceremonies and formations. For this, his pay would have been increased to $61 per month.

Sgt. Math English, extreme right, with a working party dressed in fatigues, Fort Casey, 1917. *Math English personal artifacts: Fort Casey Collection.*

Two other items in Math's footlocker from his Fort Casey years are the *Marksman A* badge and the *First Class Pistol Shot* badge. A soldier had to re-qualify annually to be authorized to wear either of these. The Marksman badge denoted a special rifle proficiency for Coast Artillery troops at a range of 200 to 600 yards, measured by slow and rapid fire, standing, kneeling, and prone, firing at both moving and fixed targets. The First Class Pistol award carried an extra pay compensation at that time of $1

Photo credit: Steven Kobylk

per month. While this sounds minimal today, in 1910, a sergeant's base pay was $39 per month.

Most of Fort Casey's fortification work was complete when Math English reported there for duty, and it remains nearly intact within the current Fort Casey State Park. Visitors today, focusing on the readily-visible waterfront gun batteries and the 1903 lighthouse, may totally overlook the mortar pits where Math was assigned. Fort Casey's two mortar batteries, Schenck and Seymour, were located on the east side of the current park entrance, to the left and down the embankment from the roadway and were nearly identical to the

149th Company Mortars in Battery Schenck Pit B, Fort Casey, Washington. *Math English personal artifacts: Fort Casey Collection.*

mortar Battery Habersham at Fort Screvens where English would have originally trained.

Each battery consisted of two concrete pits; each pit contained four 12-inch mortars. Although mortars are rather short, barreled cannons, the 40 x 50 feet pits at Fort Casey left little operational space for the 88 men needed to load, aim, and fire the four mortars simultaneously. In most cases only two mortars per pit were fired at any one time. Ammunition was stored in passageways behind doors in the pits' parapets.

Obviously, any target sailing past Fort Casey was not visible from the mortar pits. Mortar crews relied on men located in the fire control building near the lighthouse to track the targets over time, using position-finding telescopes. Those men relayed the data by telephone to another crew waiting in the plotting rooms behind the mortar batteries. The plotters, working over a huge semicircular board table, used the tracking data to determine the target's speed, range, and direction (azimuth) location, compensating for weather and other variables. They, in turn, sent the firing data to men standing by in a booth behind each pit ready to write the information on chalkboards before posting it outside the data booth where the gunner in the pit could read it. Since mortars were fired indirectly at targets (unlike guns that were fired directly at targets), crews used different weights of powder and shells, depending upon the distance to their target.

In the early days, mortars were armed and fired in salvo, the shells soaring in a high trajectory up, over the embankment, across the open field and the gun batteries, to fall theoretically on enemy ships passing through the inlet. The presumption was that firing multiple shells at one time improved the odds of accurately hitting the targets. After fire control and plotting techniques improved, mortar crews began firing directly onto the targets. Sergeant English, as a gun commander, had to master both firing techniques.

Crew of the 149th Company, Coast Artillery Corps, Fort Casey, WA firing from Battery Schenck. *Photo credit:* **Steven Kobylk Collection.**

The soldiers assigned to the Puget Sound coastal forts in the early 1900's trained constantly, plotting potential enemy targets being towed through the inlet at different speeds from different angles at all times of night or day. Most of the time they fired sub-caliber ammunition (a smaller barrel within the barrel) which saved money and kept the barrels from wearing out too fast. However, live fire was used during annual exercises when the three forts at Admiralty Inlet coordinated their drills. In 1910, the two-week-long exercise even utilized the Navy's Pacific Squadron warships to create mock naval attacks. In the early days, firing wasn't particularly accurate and those on the tugboats were somewhat at risk, but by 1913, the Forts Casey, Worden, and Flagler were among the most accurate in the nation.[5]

Docents at the fort today are proud to declare that "Fort Casey's guns were never fired in anger." However, one elderly volunteer docent loved to tell a story that may have had its basis in the 1910 court martial of 1st Lieutenant Rollo F. Anderson, CAC, the battery commander of Battery Alexander Schenck, 12-inch mortars. According to army records, the lieutenant was found guilty on one of six counts for "fail[ing] to use necessary precautions for safety, in consequence of which one of the projectiles struck the U.S. Steamer *Major Evan Thomas,* which was towing the target, injuring the vessel and greatly endangering the lives of all aboard said vessel."[6]

The docent's anecdotal version claims that the tugboat's crew had a new cook on board who was terrified when the guns starting firing at the target. The old timers laughed and hooted when the frightened man jumped overboard and started swimming toward Port Townsend on the far shore. The next thing they knew, the tugboat captain pushed them overboard and hollered down, "Don't come back without that guy. He's the best cook we've ever had."[7]

That version has not been verified, but Sergeant English would probably have been a witness to the documented account. Lieutenant Anderson's fine of $50 for two months and restriction to the post was minimal since the vessel didn't sink and no one was injured. Besides, his accuracy was really on target!

During the first six years of his tour at Fort Casey, Math English, as a single man, lived with the other soldiers on the fort. Going off-duty, he would have walked from the mortar pits to the garrison along the base of the hill, past the bakery and post exchange before angling left at the gymnasium toward the row of wood-frame barracks for enlisted men, one of which was his home until he married.

Each two-story barrack was large enough to house a full company of 109 men. Their narrow metal-framed beds, covered with wool blankets and a white pillow each, were arranged in long rows across the single room on the second floor with each man's regulation trunk or "locker" at the foot of his bed. Pillars held up the high ceilings, and numerous windows provided daylight while hanging oil lamps were used at night until electric lights were installed in 1913. Radiators heated the quarters and pot-bellied stoves provided back up. The first floor contained the kitchen and the mess hall, a day room for men off-duty, and the company offices. The latrine, shower rooms, laundry rooms, and boiler were in the basement along with storage for equipment.

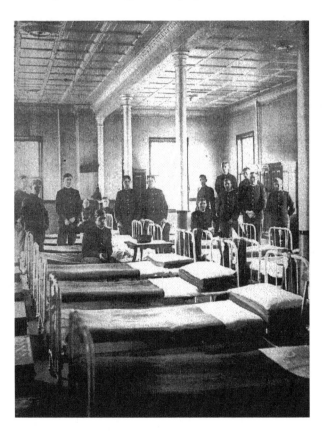

Math English, mid-background by window, probably in 149th Company Barracks #17, Fort Casey. *Math English personal artifacts: Fort Casey Collection.*

Each company had its own cook who was responsible for planning the menus, requisitioning the supplies, preparing the meals, and supervising the clean-up detail. A single bakery at the fort provided breads, pies, cakes, and cookies for the entire garrison. The base commissary stocked standard foodstuffs, but cooks might supplement their rations with fresh fruits and vegetables from the local farms or the men might bring in wild game and fish. One photo from Math's footlocker shows him with a group of friends out hunting with their rifles. The island woodlands and ponds were home to deer, geese, ducks, squirrels, and even black bear.

Individual companies usually had their own barber and tailor. Uniforms in Puget Sound were primarily made of wool, so dry cleaning was done on post by civilian contractors. If the company had extra funds, it might also send its laundry out.

The single soldiers found numerous ways to spend their off-duty hours. Competition events between companies and, at times, with soldiers from the neighboring forts included baseball games, track and field sports, tent pitching contests, and marksmanship contests. Card-playing was also popular considering all the rainy days throughout the winter months. Bands were formed, and girls from surrounding towns would be invited to dances in the gymnasium. Three-day passes could be requested for trips to Port Townsend on the Olympic Peninsula or to the mainland. Around 1914, a popular diversion included the ferry trip to the mainland where soldiers could hire a car and drive up and down the single paved lane between Everett and Seattle at fabulous speeds of 30 mph with the additional challenge of avoiding cows and horses wandering across the roadway.

Individual officers' quarters, built in modified Victorian style, were located across the parade ground. The entire garrison was in effect a small town with its own post office, an exchange selling magazines, sports gear, cigarettes, and other personal items, a hospital, a gymnasium that doubled as a theater, and a bowling alley. Its population, comprised of three companies with up to 100 men each plus additional support personnel, equaled and, at times, surpassed that of the nearest civilian community, Coupeville.

An early 20th century view of the Fort Casey garrison, showing barracks in the foreground, the parade grounds and the road to Coupeville to the left. *Photo credit: Island County Historical Society.*

Sergeant English in Coupeville, Washington

American sea captains established a small village in 1852 for their families on the sheltered shore of Penn Cove in central Whidbey Island and named it *Coupeville* in honor of Captain Thomas Coupe while settlers from the United States developed farms on the nearby prairie under the Donation Land Claim Act of 1850. The community already had several churches, a school and an academy, a post office, hotel, and various shops when troops began arriving at Fort Casey and started practicing on the big guns.

After some local residents complained that the explosions shook windows and frightened livestock, riders were sent within a two mile radius to alert farmers that firing was soon to begin so they could open doors and windows to prevent possible breakage. Many local citizens spent evenings during the annual exercises along the coastline where they could observe the interplay of searchlights and tracers.

Interaction was frequent between the town and the fort. Townspeople were allowed to use the fort hospital while the children in military families rode in horse-drawn wagons to and from the public schools they attended in Coupeville.[8] A number of Fort Casey's military families attended the Coupeville churches, and officers often encouraged enlisted men to join in. A common practice included helping the churches with maintenance and repairs during off-duty hours, thereby diverting men from visiting the saloons located just off the fort grounds around Crockett Lake. In reciprocation, the townspeople were invited to attend parades, concerts, and dances on the fort and to participate in or observe sports that included baseball, basketball, bowling, and tennis.[9] Such activities naturally brought the single soldiers into contact with the eligible young ladies of the community, and many romances developed into marriage. The Coupeville Methodist Church records show a major increase in marriages and adult baptisms after 1903 with many of the men citing "Fort Casey" as their residence.[10]

In 1909, William T. Howard purchased *The Island County Times* and moved his family from Schuyler, Nebraska to Coupeville. Mary Alice Howard, approximately 18 years old, somewhere met Sergeant English. They courted, and, on March 16, 1910, Reverend E. S. Ireland joined them in marriage at the Congregational Church on Main Street, a building which a few years later became St. Mary's Catholic Church. Mary and Math became parents of a son born on March 19, 1911 whom they named Howard.

During his years at Fort Casey, Math belonged to the Nile Temple Nobles of the Mystic Shrine in Seattle, a fraternal organization of Freemasons, better known as the "Shriners," who involved themselves in community service and charitable work. His uncle, William Logue in Gibson, Georgia, was a Mason, according to the tombstone on his grave. In Washington, Math may have been friends with the Admiralty Head lighthouse keeper, C. H. Davis, who was also a Mason and well-liked at Fort Casey. Another prominent Mason in the area was Garland Nelson Whistler, commanding officer of the Puget Sound defenses from 1908 to 1911.

According to a letter written by Dr. E. F. Ristine, a physician from Coupeville who, like Sgt. English, fought in France, he and Math together attained the 32nd degree in the Scottish Rite of freemasonry.[11] The Seattle Shriners separated from the Tacoma Temple in 1908 or 1909. Their meetings took place at the Moore Theater until the Masonic Temple was completed in 1916 in the Arcade Building in Seattle.

In order to attend these meetings, Dr. Ristine and Math would have utilized one of the steamboats in the local "mosquito fleet" that made daily runs up and down the length of Whidbey Island through the Saratoga Passage. Until the bridge at Deception Pass was built in the 1930's, residents on the island depended on privately-owned ferries and steamers to reach the mainland. Nearly every little town had its dock which did double-duty as a meeting place for neighbors to pick up their mail and meet friends. According to historian Roger Sherman, "fly on the Flyer" was a household expression for the steamer *Flyer* that made four round trips daily at 18 mph.[12]

The current pier at Coupeville was completed in 1905, no doubt to the excitement of the little community's citizens who persisted in calling it a "wharf." The Lovejoy Boat Works in town built a number of steamers which residents of Coupeville and Fort Casey regarded with affection. When the *Whidby* was launched in May, 1907, a crowd of nearly 100 gathered for a speech and christening with a wine bottle, followed by a free dance and public supper, courtesy of the Island Transportation Company.

Probably Math and his wife, Mary Alice, were as dismayed as others when the *Whidby* burned one night in Oak Harbor, killing two people. They may also have entered the naming contest for its replacement, the *Calista,* and must have traveled frequently on it. Perhaps they attended the 1909 Alaska-Yukon-Pacific Exposition in Seattle. Mary's father, as editor of the local newspaper, met the "mosquito fleet" daily and filled his columns with tidbits such as "Mrs. W. T. Howard and Mrs. M. L. English with little Howard English spent last Saturday in Everett, shopping and trying to catch a glimpse of Santa Claus."[13]

Other civic events that would have affected the lives of Math and his family include the incorporation of Coupeville as a town in 1910 for that led to the installation of electricity and telephone systems. That same year, women in Washington were allowed to vote in state elections.

In 1913, an auto ferry began operation at Deception Pass, connecting Whidbey Island to Fidalgo Island and ultimately to the mainland by road. The Island County sheriff reminded drivers in a January 1915 newspaper notice that the speed limit in towns was 12 mph and in the county 24 mph. The maximum fine for exceeding the limit was $100.

The February 26, 1915 front page of *The Island County Times* reported: "Sgt. English of Fort Casey has bought himself a new Buick auto, the first of its make so far as we can learn to be brot (sic) to this vicinity. Mr. English has accepted the agency for Island County for the Buick machine."

Math English giving 149th Co sergeants a ride on Fort Casey road in his new Buick. *Math English personal artifacts: Fort Casey Collection.*

Like any new car owner, Math enjoyed showing it off. A photo shows him in the right side driver's seat with four fellow sergeants of the 149th Company as passengers. That Model 17 came in red or blue, had a fold-down canopy, and cost around $1750.

In May, Math drove his family and in-laws to Bellingham, a distance of about sixty miles, to visit relatives, and editor Howard reported, "The trip was a delightful one, the Pacific Highway [which follows the coast] is in excellent condition and is traveled by hundreds of autos every day."[14]

Magnificent holiday feasts at Fort Casey followed an Army tradition. At Thanksgiving, the officers joined the enlisted men for dinner, but they celebrated separately at Christmas. Civilian employees at the fort and their families were invited to attend. The menus for 1915 and 1916 started with turkey or oyster soup and oyster crackers. Entrée choices included roast turkey, Westphalia ham, baked halibut, or roast pork loin accompanied by candied sweet potatoes, creamed peas, corn, lobster or crab salad and more. For dessert, there were fruit and mince pies, coconut layer cakes, apples, oranges, bananas, and nuts, and, for after-dinner—cigars, cigarettes, coffee, or bottled beer—the only time beer was allowed on post. The roster of the company lists 1st Sergeant Math L. English as the top non-commissioned officer (NCO).

The soldiers also held Christmas parties for the neighborhood school children and their parents, inviting them to the gymnasium to watch holiday skits and receive presents from old Santa himself.

In February 1916, a record snowfall covered the island for the better part of a week. Fort Casey reported 36 inches. Crews spent a whole day digging passageways between the barracks, guardhouse, quartermaster's warehouse, and the barns where horses and mules waited to be fed. The next day, they used the animals to clear the rest of the roadways at the fort.

The barracks at Fort Casey following the record snowfall of February 1916. *Photo credit: Island Count Historical Society.*

Life for soldiers and their families at Fort Casey was good during the early years of its operation. After duty hours, the men enjoyed their clubs and sports. The wives cared for their children and participated in social and church activities. But events beyond the Atlantic Ocean, in Europe and the Middle East, would too soon disrupt their pacific idyll.

Sergeant English Goes to War

In the summer of 1914, the residents of Whidbey Island were, for the most part, quietly going about their business, growing wheat, milking dairy cattle, running their shops, raising their families. The soldiers at Fort Casey practiced with the heavy guns, played baseball with the town teams, danced with the girls of Coupeville, and laughed and shouted at the silent movies being shown at the local theater. For news in those days before radio or television, folks relied on word-of-mouth or telephone, personal letters, and the weekly edition of the *Island County Times*. Events of national or international import, transmitted via telegraph, might rate a corner of the local paper's front page, but more often, appeared on inside pages.

It is likely that few in Coupeville knew or cared that some archduke and his wife were assassinated in a far-off city called Sarajevo. Surrounded by the silent mountains and the tranquil, sparkling waters of Puget Sound, they would never dream that four and a half years later, men from their peaceful community would lie buried in the plains of France, having fought in the war that was sparked by those assassin's bullets.

A century later, we still ask, just what happened that led to war? The answer is lost among the tangle of international treaties binding the nations of Europe like the coils of barbed wire along the trenches—secret promises between countries to defend each other if attacked—and at the very core of the matter, those universal human flaws of greed for wealth, desire for power, animosity, fear, and national pride.

The details have been recorded in countless books. It is sufficient for our story to know that Germany under Kaiser Wilhelm invaded Belgium and France, and that England was allied with the French along a battle front extending some 650 miles from the North Sea to Switzerland.

For almost three years, President Woodrow Wilson resisted involving America in Europe's conflict. But when Germany commenced unrestricted submarine attacks in the Atlantic Ocean, endangering American shipping and lives, he decided it was time for Congress to declare war on the side of England and France.

America was far from ready to join the battle. She had some National Guard units and a small Regular Army which included Fort Casey's Coast Artillery Corps, but she lacked sufficient trained officers, equipment, material, and manpower. While a national lottery was created primarily to draft men into the infantry, the War Department sought for the necessary leaders from among non-commissioned officers who were familiar with heavy guns such as those at Fort Casey—men like First Sergeant Math English who had an excellent service record. Furthermore, Math may have felt the war offered an opportunity to advance his fifteen-year career.

One week after Congress declared war on April 6, 1917, one hundred NCOs from Forts Casey, Worden, and Flagler departed for Officers' Training School (OTS) at the Presidio in San Francisco. Math English was among the 21 from Fort Casey.[15]

On June 8, 1917, he received his commission as a 2nd Lieutenant. The oath that he took had been revised following the Civil War. It read:

> I,...do solemnly swear (or affirm) that I will support and defend the Constitution of the United States against all enemies, foreign or domestic; that I will bear true faith and allegiance to the same; that I take this obligation freely, without any mental reservation or purpose of evasion; and that I will well and faithfully discharge the duties of the office on which I am about to enter. So help me God.

It is reasonable to assume he was granted a few days' furlough—the term meaning *leave* in those days—to visit family before joining the 7th Regiment, 2nd Battalion in Fort Adams, Rhode Island. Farewells are bittersweet. Math, his wife, Mary Alice, and six-year-old son, Howard, no doubt tried to fill their time together with happy memories to sustain themselves in the days ahead. Perhaps they walked along the beach at Ebey's Landing or picnicked along Penn Cove. Maybe the Howards held a big family dinner and gave Math gifts of clothing or food to take with him.

Too soon, the day of departure would arrive with both agony and relief. Military wives in any generation wish to postpone the break as long as possible on one hand, while on the other, they feel relief when the day of separation has finally passed. They will be the ones left with loneliness and an empty place while their men have little time to miss home, faced as they are with new places, new people, and new duties.

No one knows what Mary Alice did with Math's letters home, but her father, W. T. Howard, as owner and editor of the Coupeville newspaper, frequently included excerpts of letters from "the boys." After all, it was his business to let people know what was going on "over there," and he obviously felt some pride in having one son in the Signal Corps in Mississippi, plus two sons and two sons-in-law "Somewhere in France."

John E. Herrett, son of Mr. and Mrs. G. I. Herrett of Ebey's Prairie, described the soldiers' journey across the nation in a New Year's Day letter, 1918. The account published in *The Island County Times* noted: "It is just five months ago today since we boarded the train at American Lake and began the trip which brot (sic) us here. We were an enthusiastic company at that time and enjoyed to the fullest every moment of our trip. Many of us viewed for the first time the great cities of our central states, the Hudson river, the tall buildings of New York, and our last view of our country—The Statue of Liberty."

Newly-commissioned Lieutenant English apparently spent most of July 1917 at Fort Adams, established at the mouth of Narragansett Bay about the time of the War of 1812 to protect the entrance to Newport Harbor, and a century later, one of the Coastal Artillery Corps facilities like Fort Casey in Washington. Considering the short time that Math was there, it was probably being used as a staging area for deployment of the Heavy Artillery Units to France. Math made the acquaintance of Edmund N. Hébert, a fellow officer and corpsman, and the two became close friends. They would both eventually join the Tanks Corps under Colonel George S. Patton, Jr., and Hébert would write a lengthy letter of condolence to Math's widow after the war ended.[16]

Sometime in August, Math's unit sailed for Europe. Most troop ships departed from New York City with thousands of soldiers crowding the decks, waving to the exuberant crowds on the pier below. George M. Cohen captured the bravado, the patriotic confidence in youthful invincibility with his popular song, "Send the word over there, That the Yanks are coming, the Yanks are coming…." The French and the English in "the old country" had struggled for three years without defeating the Kaiser's "Huns" or "Boches" as the Germans were derogatorily called, and American

"Yanks" planned to show them how victory was won, vowing "we won't come back till it's over over there."

Traveling in convoys as protection from German U-boats, the ships spent about a week in transit towards ports at Bordeaux, La Rochelle, St. Nazaire, or Le Havre in France while some stopped over temporarily in England. The men spent their time playing cards, writing letters, and bonding with each other. Few really comprehended what the future held.

Before the Americans arrived in 1917, the belligerents were literally entrenched on the battlefields. Germany's trenches along the Hindenburg Line were primarily concrete structures linked together for miles underground, wired with electricity and telephones in places, with kitchens, dining rooms, and sleeping areas besides the front line fighting sections.

By contrast, the British and French trenches were open pits, as much as ten feet deep, the walls braced with corrugated iron or wooden slats, the floors often muddy rivers from the spring and autumn rains. They ran zig-zag across miles of fields with a No-Man's Land between the enemies, former farm and pasture land pock-marked by three years' of bombardment. Any trees still standing were leafless, jagged stumps pointing skyward.

Along both sides, men hunkered around machine guns protected by coils of barbed wire, strafing infantrymen charging "over the top" in attack. By 1916, the front moved forward or backward by feet or yards rather than miles, and the war had reached a stalemate. Thousands had lost their lives, but neither side could claim victory or would surrender.

The British and French hoped to replenish their losses with American soldiers, but General John J. Pershing, U.S. Commander-in-Chief was determined that his men would only fight as a separate American unit, the American Expeditionary Forces (A.E.F.).

After disembarking in Europe, the fresh American troops were shuttled by trains which they called the *40-8's* (forty men or eight horses) to various military installations throughout France for additional training before entering combat.

French *carte postale* showing US Tank Corps officers "somewhere in France," 1918. Captain English is standing in the back row, second from the left. *Math English personal artifacts: Fort Casey Collection.*

Lieutenants English and Hébert from the Coast Artillery Corps were first assigned where guns like those used at Fort Casey were mounted on railroad cars to be rolled into battle. On the back of a postcard showing such a gun, Math's son wrote, "Father went over with the heavy railroad artillery. Was transferred to drilling men. Then he asked to be transferred to the Heavy tanks (to get action.)"[17]

By most accounts, newly-arrived American officers had considerable free time, studying procedures with the French during the day and going to bistros or the French Officers' Clubs to eat and drink in the evenings or staying in the barracks writing letters that often began, "I don't have much to write about...." Saturdays and Sundays were their days off.

Math wrote to his wife of visiting one of France's famed walled cities and attending Sunday services in its cathedral. In accordance with security regulations, he avoided naming specific towns and historical sites. In fact, one of his duties as an officer would have been to censor his subordinates' letters, blotting out details that would reveal troop locations, strength, or plans.

There are several walled cities in the region where Math was assigned, but few with cathedrals as well. He may have gone to Bourges, south of Paris, or to Autun where he might have examined the medieval fortifications, comparing them to the stone walls used at Fort Adams or the dirt embankments at Fort Casey. In a somber comment, he wrote that at the cathedral mass "all of a thousand women were present and practically every one in mourning for some relative lost in the war."[18]

In another letter, written in October, 1917, Math sent his wife two Liberty bonds with comments about the enthusiasm with which the young privates in the Army kept only $3 pocket money each month in order to send their wives, parents, or sweethearts bonds costing $30 each.[19]

At Christmas time, 1917, he probably received one of the packages sent from the Coupeville "Round Table Club." The local Red Cross chapter also solicited donations to be used sending "one dollar's worth" of goodies to "every soldier in Uncle Sam's service now in camp in the United States." Their plea, published in *The Island County Times* on December 7, echoed the words of General Pershing who had declared, "Germany can be beaten, Germany must be beaten, Germany will be beaten!" The ladies stated, "We can give each soldier a Christmas present, we must give each soldier a Christmas present, we shall give each soldier a Christmas present."

That same newspaper issue continued with directions for dropping off the donations of money or items at Benson's restaurant and included a list: envelopes, pencils, Boy Scout knives, neckties, mouth organs, electric torches, compasses, playing cards, tobacco, pipes, cigaret (sic) papers, water tight match boxes, chewing gum, sweetened crackers in original package, fruit cake, salted nuts, prunes, figs, dates, raisins, hard candy, chocolate in tin foil, licorice."

The ladies were determined that "Island County will do her share, if not a little more, and be happy in the thought that every boy in our Army and Navy no matter how lonely or friendless he may be, will have his heart warmed and lightened at the blessed Christmas-tide by the receipt of a Christmas present from his fellow countrymen."

The Island County Times printed a "thank you" on the front page of its February 15, 1918 issue from a James W. Torrence. The formality of his letter is typical of other soldiers' letters written during that war. He wrote:

> Such expressions of devotion and service
> from the loved ones at home serve only as an
> inspiration and vindication that our cause is just,
> and tends to a fuller realization that the people
> at home are as truly patriots as we who are on
> foreign soil.

Lieutenant English Joins the Tank Corps

On January 1, 1918, Lieutenant Math English received transfer orders to the American Expeditionary Forces Tank Corps under the command of then-Colonel Samuel D. Rockenbach. Tanks were a new addition to the arsenal of armed warfare being developed to overcome the stalemate of trench warfare with mobility. They were inspired, according to tank lore, by the Holt Caterpillar tractors manufactured to run on continuous crawler tracks, first in Stockton, California and later, in Walla Walla, Washington. The British Lieutenant-Colonel E. S. Swinton had promoted the concept of a "land battleship" rolling on crawler tracks, thereby resulting in the use of nautical terminology such as hulls and hatches. The name *tank* however, gained popularity for its brevity. Besides, comparing the strange contraptions to water tanks camouflaged their real purpose.

With the support of Winston Churchill, Lord of the Admiralty, the British had designed the Mark series of heavy tanks and used them for the first time September 15, 1916 at the Battle of the Somme, reputedly causing panic among the unsuspecting Germans who fled from the onslaught. The French also developed a lighter Renault tank. Although America was designing its own version of the new weapon, the war ended before any reached France.

The organization and training in France of America's First Tank Corps was assigned to George S. Patton, Jr., a 1909 graduate from West Point. Patton had first experienced combat as a cavalry soldier along the Mexican-American border in 1916 when a patrol of soldiers, including Patton serving as General John Pershing's aide-de-camp, took three automobiles from Fort Bliss into Mexico on a punitive action against Pancho Villa and his band. Three Mexicans were killed in the brief skirmish while Patton's men escaped injury.

Hearing that an American tanks corps was being created, Captain Patton, among the first A.E.F. officers to reach France in 1917, applied by reminding General Pershing of that first motorized attack by Americans. That feat, along with Patton's fluency in French, led to his assignment at Bourg, France to establish a tank training facility after completing his personal two-weeks' training with the French.[20]

When Math English volunteered for the Tank Corps, Patton was in the process of setting up the school for the new tank battalions coming to Bourg near the town of Langres. One of Patton's first tasks was to determine how many men were needed for a tank battalion, ranging from the drivers and gunners down to the mechanics and kitchen crew. Estimating that he would need 18 officers, 331 enlisted men, 77 tanks, and 42 wheeled vehicles per battalion, he then set to work planning tactics, missions, and the curriculum to train his tankers.

Lt. Col. George S. Patton, Jr. in France, commander of 1st/304th Tank Brigade. U.S. Signal Corps photo # 17592.

Throughout this war, commanders considered tanks as support for the infantry. The tanks would initiate an assault, smashing machine gun nests and barbed wire, forging pathways across the trenches, and generally, smoothing the way for infantry "doughboys" to rush "over the top" into combat.

Lieutenant Math English arrived at the Bourg Training Center about January 8, 1918, along with seven other officers recruited from the Coast Artillery Corps (C.A.C.) enlisted ranks. By-then-Major Patton still had no tanks for training purposes, so he began drilling the men with physical fitness exercises and communication procedures. Tank design seated the driver low in front while the gunner sat above him. Both had only narrow openings through which to look outside, so a third soldier stood on top in a turret where he had 360° of vision. His job was to send directions below. The rumble and clanking sounds of the tank, compounded by reconnaissance airplanes overhead, shells bursting nearby, and machine gun bullets pinging off the metal, would make voice contact virtually impossible, so the crew worked out a system that they called "machine foot signals." A kick on the left shoulder meant turn left, on the right, turn right, on the head, stop!

Patton also enforced strict military discipline and expected his officers to require the same. He believed that immaculate personal appearance and the execution of crisp military salutes strengthened troop morale and pride. Also determined that his tankers would develop a strong bond within the Corps, he instituted several plans to achieve it. He designed a smart-looking uniform with colorful shoulder patches, Sam Browne belts, and trimmer overcoats, then introduced a soft, brimless military cap or *kepi* for officers. Matt's wool cap is in the footlocker donated to Fort Casey.

Math probably participated with his fellow officers developing tank corps insignia as another part of Patton's morale-building program. Patton issued instructions: "I want a shoulder insignia. We claim to have the fire power of artillery, the mobility of cavalry, and the ability to hold ground of the infantry, so whatever you come up with, it must have red, yellow, and blue in it."[21] The officers also designed collar devices—a tank in profile surrounded by a wreath to be worn, one on each side of the neck opening, with tanks facing each other.

World War I Tank Corps left side collar device belonging to Captain English. *Math English personal artifacts: Fort Casey Collection.*

In the spring of 1918, Math wrote to his wife that Company C under his command had been picked as best in the regiment to present an exhibition drill for General Pershing and his staff. Math considered it an honor to receive Pershing's personal compliment regarding the quality of his unit.[22]

On March 23, 1918, the French finally delivered ten light Renault tanks to Patton's school, and training could begin in earnest. Each man was expected to learn all the jobs related to operating and maintaining a tank. Maneuvering the caterpillar tracks up and over steep grades tended to be the trickiest skill to develop for the nose would rise high into the air until it seemed the tank would tip over, then its nose would drop until the tracks took hold of earth again and the driver could apply the gas and move forward.

Math wrote to his wife that the tanks did not make as good time as did the Buick he owned while at Fort Casey, but that one will "go anywhere, thru (sic) barbed wire, entanglements, over ditches and other obstacles, and if it happens to turn upside down rambles right along."[23] He also wrote that the dust stirred up by the tanks so hurt his eyes that he was given a six-day furlough to recuperate.

Excerpts of the letter describing his trip to the French Riviera appeared in *The Island County Times* dated June 7, 1918. He wrote to his wife that he and an old Fort Casey friend by the name of Brown were relaxing along the southern coast of France, visiting resorts at Nice, Marseilles, and Monaco. Math was especially impressed by the gambling casino, Monte Carlo, and its paraphernalia although as a uniformed soldier he was prohibited from participating. The area around Nice reminded him of California with its flowers, lemons, and oranges, and while most food seemed plentiful, he noted a shortage of sugar. He told Mary that he had sent her some cards from Italy—views of the coastline—and states that he's getting quite a collection of views.

Hints of homesickness crept into his sentences—"Living is not so high as it was in the states when I left. I have been stopping at a hotel and it only cost me $3 for room and board. The same meals would have cost more than that in Seattle when I left there, which seems to me a life time."

He continued, "Well, dear, I have had a fairly good time since here, been going out somewhere every day into the mountains on the train as I can't stay on the beach on account of my eyes. Am wearing shadow glasses, but my eyes don't seem to get much better. Don't think the Mediterranean sun is very good for them as it is the brightest I ever saw."

One of his train trips followed the Grande Corniche Road built by Napoleon between Menton on the Italian border and Nice. He told Mary, "It is about 30 miles along the ridge of mountains and is supposed to be the most scenic trip in France. It overlooks the Mediterranean and reminds me a good deal of the Cascades, only the slopes of these mountains are all terraced and planted in olive trees, which makes one of the most beautiful bits of scenery I have ever yet seen. Part of the road is an old Roman road and there are lots of old ruins. I know that if you were ever to come here to see them, there would be no getting you away."

By early June, 1918, Patton had enough trained men to organize a second light tank battalion. Math's friend, Edmund Hébert, was made the adjutant of the new battalion while Math remained in the 1st Battalion and was made commander of the new Company C. On July 1, 1918, Math was promoted to Captain. The reorganized units continued training with the addition of battlefield exercises through most of the summer.

The Tank Corps Engages in Combat[24]

Finally, seventeen months after America declared war on Germany, the American Expeditionary Forces, including General Rockenbach's newly-created Tank Corps, were scheduled to enter combat attacking the St. Mihiel Salient on September 12. This V-shaped protrusion of the German lines into France lay south of the major French and British battlefields, almost due east of Paris, near Verdun and the city of Metz.

Captain English's men were in the 326th Battalion which was later re-numbered as the 344th Battalion. His chain of command was Major Sereno E. Brett, Battalion Commander, Colonel George S. Patton, Jr., 1st Tank Brigade, General S. D. Rockenbach, 1st Tank Corps, General John Pershing, A.E.F. Commander-in-Chief.

The plan called for Math's company to support the 1st Infantry Division attacking across the *Rupt de Mad* River just north of the village of Xivray-Marvoisin. The tanks were to assemble during the night of September 11 under complete darkness and strict silence. No lights of any kind, not even cigarettes. Speak only when necessary, and then in a whisper. Rain had been falling continuously for five days, but the men kept preparing their tanks and weapons, trying not to slosh too loudly in the mud as they worked. By 1 a.m.

on September 12, all but one company of the 1st Tank Brigade were in position for the 5 a.m. attack.

Determined that no tank was to be surrendered or abandoned to the enemy, Patton admonished his troops, "Remember, you are the first American tanks. You must establish the fact the AMERICAN TANKS DO NOT SURRENDER...This is our BIG CHANCE; WHAT WE HAVE WORKED FOR...MAKE IT WORTH WHILE." [emphasis in original].[25]

Each tank had an identifying symbol painted on its turret, based on the suits of a deck of playing cards. Each platoon in Math's Company C identified its tanks by painting either a spade, club, heart, or diamond in black on a diamond-shaped background of white.

A tank from the 326th Light Tank Battalion, Company C in a muddy trench, September 12, 1918, near Seicheprey, France. *Photo credit: US Army Signal Corps.*

American heavy artillery started a four-hour barrage during the night, and at dawn, approximately 6 a.m., the tanks started rolling. Battlefield communications were primitive by 21st century standards. The most modern technology of that time was the telephone. A soldier would leave headquarters carrying a large spool of wire on his back and unroll it as he walked. After the phone lines ran out, he relied on runners to carry hand-written messages.

Initially the tanks tried signals using flags in the naval tradition, but the flags were quickly shredded. Some units carried homing pigeons in baskets into battle, but the poor birds were afraid to fly amid the sounds of gunfire and those that did were quickly shot down.

With so little means of communication, each tank crew was given an ultimate destination prior to departure and was told to move in that general direction unless it received new orders. The commanders like Math were expected to reconnoiter ahead of the tanks and, when necessary, walk in front of them directing them by hand signals over trenches, through woods and streams, and around boulders. At St. Mihiel, they encountered trenches eight feet deep and from ten to fourteen feet wide, sometimes filled with water. Even so-called light tanks became mired in the mud. Meanwhile, the Germans blanketed the area with machine gun fire and mortars.

By 7:20 a.m. on the 12th of September, Colonel Patton reported sixteen tanks in heavy fighting under thick fog and smoke cover. He trudged on foot from skirmish to skirmish, village to village, giving directions and encouragement, hitching an occasional ride on a tank. Despite mechanical breakdowns and waiting for fuel sleds to catch up, the tanks pushed forward, while infantry followed in their wake.

By about 3 p.m. on the 12th, German opposition had lessened. Twenty-five tanks of the 326th Battalion had reached the village of Nonsard, a distance of about eight miles from their morning start point. Major Brett recalled having seen his company commanders, including Captain English, standing exposed to enemy fire, directing their tank drivers and gunners amid the acrid smoke.

On that same afternoon, Patton encountered Brigadier General Douglas MacArthur observing the battle from atop a small hill. Patton admitted later that he was scared while they talked amid the gunfire, but was determined not to show it. Nevertheless, he blinked first, and MacArthur offered the assurance, "You never hear the one that gets you."[26]

The attack was delayed on the second day, September 13, while the tanks waited for fuel supplies to arrive. By 2 p.m. when the fuel reached the 326th, the Germans had essentially retreated. Major Brett sent his tanks toward Vigneulles where they assembled by midnight.

The next morning, 51 tanks started north in search of American infantry to support. A few German airplanes fired briefly on them, so Patton directed the tanks to hide in the woods and wait for further orders. There were a few more skirmishes, but apparently Math's Company C was not involved. The Battle of St. Mihiel officially ended by 9 p.m. on September 14 and the American Tank Corps was ordered to assemble at Bois de la Hazelle where they would be transported by rail to the Meuse-Argonne region.

The new Tank Corps had been tested and proven. General Rockenbach was pleased with the corps's *esprit*. His major concern was that his officers had left their headquarters to participate in the fray. Only company commanders like Math and those of lower rank were to be in the thick of the battle. Patton was admonished to stay out of immediate danger. A futile command as the next battle would reveal.

Renault tanks of the 1st Brigade moving into action near Boureuilles, France on September 26, 1918. Photo credit: US Signal Corps.

The Meuse-Argonne Campaign Begins - September 26, 1918 [27]

The A.E.F. had just over two weeks to move from the salient of St. Mihiel region north to the Argonne Forest and the River Meuse, about sixty miles, before the next major campaign was scheduled to begin. There would be little time for the battle-weary to rest.

Lieutenant Harvey Harris of the 345th Tank Battalion wrote to his parents describing days of nothing but canned corned beef hash and coffee for meals, incessant rain, cold nights, mail call disappointments when no letters came and exhilaration whenever a bundle of eight or nine letters finally arrived. News from home was more nourishing than food.[28]

The American Army was assigned to push northward along about 20 miles of the front near the town of Varennes with the Argonne Forest on the west and the Meuse River on the east. Reconnaissance revealed rugged, wooded terrain with high bluffs east of the river, streams, and deep shell craters which would hamper tank movement. So, as part of Patton's 1st Tank Brigade, the 344th Battalion under Major Sereno Brett and including Captain Math English's Company C positioned its 69 Renault tanks between

Boureuilles and Vauquois Hill south of Cheppy Woods on the evening of September 25.

"on the way to action"...Renaults of the 326/344th Tank Battalion near Boureuilles, France on September 26, 1918. *U.S. Signal Corps photo # 31858.*

Heavy artillery began softening the target at 11:30 p.m. with occasional flashes of light followed by the rumble of mortars hurling through the air. At 2:30 a.m., they began a constant barrage. For three hours, the manmade thunderstorm reverberated through the night while infantry doughboys and tankers alike hunkered in their trenches, nerves taut with anticipation, listening to the overture of the "big show." Veterans of St. Mihiel probably prayed. Trained but untested men perhaps questioned their own courage. All knew that the day dawning might be their last.

Promptly at 5:30 a.m.—H-hour—signal whistles blew and the massed troops leaped up and rushed over the top, out of the trenches into No-Man's-Land. The early daylight barely pierced the morning fog and the hovering clouds of artillery smoke. Math and his platoon leaders led the way on foot, picking the best routes for the tanks to take across the maze of trenches, some as wide as eight to ten feet and just as deep. The infantry followed behind the tanks.

As the Germans realized the attack was underway, their machine-gunners filled the air with bullets. Several American units began to suffer casualties, but Captain English's Company C initially traversed an area well-battered by the night's barrage and found little resistance. They did, however, encounter a minefield, and used the abandoned German "Danger" signs to guide themselves safely through.

Waiting behind the lines for action reports as he had been ordered to do, Colonel Patton, former cavalry officer, was "chomping at the bit" to rush forward and see the action firsthand. By 6:30 a.m., he could restrain himself no more. Gathering a group of runners to carry telephone wires and baskets of carrier pigeons, he set off on foot, his signature walking stick in one hand.

Near the village of Cheppy, the tanks and soldiers moved back and forth in confusion searching for their commanders through the fog. Suddenly a burst of enemy machine gun fire scattered them, and Colonel Patton with his group of runners sheltered within a railroad cut. Doughboys lay flattened on a hillside, below the rain of bullets. Then the fog lifted, revealing a line of tanks at the bottom of the hill, its lead tank stuck while trying to cross one of the deep trenches, blocking the path.

Furious with the inaction, Patton charged down the hill and joined Captain English in removing picks and shovels that were attached to the tank's exterior and handing them to the cowering infantrymen, ordering them to dig and get the machines moving. Math and Colonel Patton stood together on the parapet of the trench, directing the action as the men chained five tanks together and gained the necessary traction to move forward.[29]

At a later date, Patton would recommend Captain Math L. English for the Distinguished Service Cross, writing, "During the attack on Cheppy, Captain English dismounted from his tank and, under heavy machine-gun fire, personally supervised the cutting of a passage for his tanks through three hostile trenches."[30]

As for his own actions, according to his grandson, Robert H. Patton, Colonel Patton speculated, "I think I killed one man here— an American soldier. He would not work so I hit him over the head with a shovel." No one else ever documented the incident.[31]

While Math trod forward, leading his company of tanks, Patton and the men with him again hugged the ground to evade a fresh barrage of machine gun fire. Since childhood, little Georgie Patton had doubted whether his courage was worthy of his ancestors —cousins, uncles, grandparents who faced death "always willing and wishing to obtain the desirable end." [32]

He later described that morning, saying that he saw the faces of those ancestors in the clouds above the battlefield. He told himself, "It is time for another Patton to die," stood up and waved his walking stick, calling out, "Who's coming with ME?" before following Math's line of Company C tanks.[33]

A few paces forward and Patton was struck in the groin. His orderly, Private Joseph Angelo, saved his life by pulling him into a sheltered mortar crater and tying up the wound to stop the bleeding. For Patton, and to his everlasting regret, the war was over.[34] He was evacuated to an emergency treatment center and eventually to a field hospital where he spent several weeks.

Meanwhile the battle for Cheppy continued until about 1:30 when Americans secured the village. Two hours later, Captain English arrived with only two operable tanks to join the nine tanks from Company A already there. The eleven tanks from the 344th Battalion proceeded toward the town of Very to assist the infantry and French tanks battling there while Captain English set off on foot, searching for the rest of his company and leading them to Very where they spent the night.

Colonel Patton's brigade lost 43 tanks on September 26. By the end of the second day, only 83 tanks were operational. Infantry units were directed to place requests for support from the greatly-reduced tank units as needed while they pushed on toward their original objective. The extended battle allowed time for the Germans to move in re-enforcements on the third day, including anti-tank guns. Fighting was fierce and the infantry were worn out, having had little rest or food since the assault began.

Nevertheless Captain English's men, with tanks combined from Companies A and C, attacked at Baulny, wearing their masks since they had received reports that the Germans were using gas in the area. The tankers reached Exermont—their first day's objective, but pulled back since the infantry was too weak to continue. A.E.F. Headquarters expected the Germans to counterattack, so Math's tanks were ordered to hold the line from Baulny to Eclisfontaine, but no action occurred.

On September 30, the 1st Brigade tanks were recalled behind the lines for maintenance and repairs. Math and his company had fought in dust and smoke without rest, without showers, with limited rations for five continuous days. Their clothing and hair were filled with lice. Fifty-three percent of the men were wounded or killed, including Colonel Patton and four of the six captains. Thus far, Math had escaped harm, but the Americans had only pushed the German line back about four miles.

The October 4 Attack[35]

After three days of maintenance and repair, Patton's 1st Tank Corps Brigade had 89 tanks ready to return to battle. With the time of engagement set for dawn on October 4, throughout the preceding evening, the narrow French country roads were packed with vehicles —hundreds of trucks, artillery, staff cars all driven without headlights toward the front. The infantry marched in columns of twos, sitting along the ditches at times to let the tanks pass by.

Once the tanks were in position, there was time for the crews to nap or sit together talking, hoping to push aside the knowledge that on the morrow, they would enter what they called "Death Valley" between Charpentry and Baulny and some would not return. One of the younger officers with Math, Lieutenant Harvey Harris, noted that after days of constant bombardment, the night was strangely quiet. Then, to the joy of the waiting men, a mail truck arrived. In Harvey's words:

> …the greatest thing that can happen to a fellow
> is to get a bunch of mail before going over
> in an attack. Just to forget everything—gas
> up, oiling, plan of attack and the like—and
> sit down on a stump away from the bunch,
> lite (sic) up a cigarette and read the mail."[36]

The fighting over the next six and a half weeks would be intense both physically and mentally. Although the Armistice was signed on November 11, Lt. Harris waited until the evening of December 10 to write an account of the battle for his parents. Someone was playing songs on a graphaphone—*Mother MacCree, Perfect Day,* and *Silver Threads Among the Gold*—as Harris wrote, "My thots…come back to 'what are the folks doing to-nite'—and to the last time I heard music that made a lasting impression on me."[37] He recalled the excitement of receiving mail about 10 p.m. on the night of October 3, before the barrage and dawn attack were scheduled to begin.

> The war was forgotten. Then we thot of the Boche piano we'd salvaged. One of the Lts. has a wonderful tenor, and he sang wonderfully—the same pieces we're playing to-nite. Picture it! Just his voice, and no other sound—with light accompaniment. I'll wager there wasn't a man but was around that piano—with thots you can well imagine. There wasn't a day since we first went over here that we hadn't had casualties, and a lot of their buddies had been bumped off. While Doug was singing, a courier arrived; the 35th Division was being relieved and we were going over at 5:30 with the 1st Bn! Now we'll go! After planning and disposing of different things that had to be done—we turned in for a couple of hours—under a sheet iron roof we had improvised. Capt. English and Lt. [Robert C.] Llewelyn—both killed the next morning—were most optimistic. They'd made reconnaissance that afternoon." [38]

We'll never know the thoughts that buoyed Math's spirits that night. The introduction of tanks as weapons had broken the gridlock of years of trench warfare. The Germans were slowly but surely being pushed back. Allied victory seemed within reach; many were predicting that the war would be over by the next summer.

Also rumors were being circulated that some tank officers would soon be returned to the States to become trainers. Math must certainly have thought he would be included, for he had written to his family that he hoped to be home for Christmas. Fifteen months had passed since he said good-by to Mary Alice and his six-year-old son, Howard. How much the boy would have grown! And how ready Math would have felt to exchange the dirt and din of battle, the jagged tree stumps, the stench of death for the crisp, clean air of Whidbey Island, the deep blue water, the stately fir and pine, and the two snow-topped sentinels, Mount Rainier and Mount Baker, standing watch over Fort Casey and Puget Sound.

At dawn on October 4, the artillery barrage shattered the quiet night to drown out the rumble of tank engines firing up. The armored machines rolled forward at 5:20, passing American machine guns shooting as fast as the gunners could reload. The infantry had already gone over the top.

At a signal, platoons of five tanks each fanned out across the battlefield, clearing enemy machine gun nests and proceeding toward their pre-arranged objective. Company commanders, Captain English, Lieutenant Harris, and others led the way on foot with three to four runners who would carry messages back to the tank drivers. Harris noted that the German counter-barrage was "more terrible, yet wonderful than any experience before…shells falling at a rate of 20-30 a minute."[39] About 10 a.m., an orderly ran up to Harris with the sad report that Captain English, at the head of his company of tanks, had been killed just a few minutes earlier.

Colonel George S. Patton, Jr. later reported that Math's tanks encountered especially rough terrain in the area of the Bois de Montrebeau less than a mile south of Exermont.[40] His second citation for the Distinguished Service Cross for extraordinary heroism in action states that "Captain English left his tank under heavy machine-gun and artillery fire to make a personal reconnaissance, in the course of which he was killed."[41]

For Math, the war was over. The A.E.F., along with British and French forces would continue fighting right up until the eleventh hour on the eleventh day of the eleventh month—November 11, 1918—when the Germans surrendered and the Armistice was signed at a railroad siding near Compiègne, France.

Condolences and Recognition

Like many families across the United States, Math's wife, son, and in-laws rejoiced that the end of the war meant their loved one would be returning home. They anticipated a happy Christmas reunion. Then, two weeks later, their hopes were dashed. The War Department's telegram arrived in Coupeville on November 29, reporting the death of Captain Math L. English, Tank Corps, A.E.F.

Math was buried first near the field where he fell, northeast of Exermont.   After the Armistice, Dr. Ristine, Math's Masonic friend from Coupeville who was serving with the 139th Infantry Medical Corps near Koblenz, Germany, searched for and located the government cross marking Math's grave near Exermont. He

designed and made a second cross documenting Math's ties to the Coast Artillery Corps and to the 32° Lawson Consistory of Seattle.[42] When the Meuse-Argonne American Cemetery at Romagne, France was developed, Math's remains were transferred to Plot A, Row 7, Grave 26.

Mary Howard English, Math's widow, received three exceptional letters of condolence. On October 29, 1918, Math's commanding officer wrote:

> My dear Madam:
>
> Words are useless as a means of comforting you for the great loss and sorrow which has come into your life, due to the death of your gallant husband, Captain Math L. English, Tank Corps, U.S. Army. It may, however, help ameliorate your grief to realize in what very high esteem Captain English was held by all the officers and men with whom he

came into contact. I believe that the Brigade is unanimous in attributing to him all the highest virtues of a man and officer.

I take the liberty of reciting the following action of Captain English, which you and his children should always guard as a perfect example of heroism and soldierly devotion to duty under the most trying circumstances. On the 26th September, 1918, at a point about two miles south of Cheppy, on the Aire River, it was necessary to move some tanks across some very difficult trenches.

To carry out this manoeuver we were forced to dig a passage over the trenches under the direct and murderous fire of German machine guns, at a range of less than 300 yards. In order to hearten his men and to properly supervise the digging, your husband stood on the parapet for over 15 minutes and with death and destruction raining all about him, he, by his calm and fearless bearing, inspired the men and carried to a successful termination his difficult task.

In my own experience I have never seen, and I have yet to hear of a more heroic exhibition of devotion to duty and scorn of death.

Please allow me, my dear Madam, to close, again assuring you of my heartfelt sympathy for you and my unbounded admiration for your gallant husband.

I have the honor to remain,

> Very respectfully,
>
> (signed)
>
> GEORGE S. PATTON, JR.
> Colonel, Tank Corps,
> Commanding 1st Brigade.[43]

Mrs. Beatrice Ayers Patton, wife of Colonel Patton, mailed a hand-written note on black-edged stationery and envelope, postmarked November 28, 1918, 5 p.m. from Pride's Crossing, Massachusetts:

My dear Mrs. English—

Colonel Patton has written me of your husband's great gallantry and of the irreparable loss of his death. I must add my sympathy to his. I know what your grief is, but never let it overshadow your pride in him. Your children have the finest inheritance any children could have—a Father who gave his life for his Country.

With all sympathy for you and yours, believe me,

Most sincerely,

(signed: Beatrice Ayer Patton)

———————

Mrs. George S. Patton Jr.[44]

The third condolence was printed on a notecard and personally signed by John J. Pershing, Commander-in-Chief of the American Expeditionary Forces.[45]

In addition, the Recorder of the Masonic Nile Temple of the Mystic Shrine in Seattle, Frank B. Lazier, wrote to Mary English on December 18, 1918, telling her that a gold star in Math's honor had been placed on their order's service flag. His letter includes expressions of patriotism typically made during the Great War, later referred to as World War I:

…we only learned but lately that your good husband, Capt. M. L. English, had made the supreme sacrifice, and given "the last full measure of devotion" that our country might be free from danger of foreign domination and that the peoples of the world might in the future, tenderly remember all those who had sacrificed their lives that they and their children might enjoy the fruits of liberty and equality and be free for all time from the brutalities of autocracy and militarism. And so they and so we, will look upon your dear husband, who laid down his life in our behalf.[46]

The obituary in the *Nile News*, February 1919, noted that Math's "character and habits were above reproach, and a cleaner, better man, or one who entertained a higher or more conscientious regard for duty, never lived."

Math's close friend, Captain Edmund Hébert, likewise attested to the esteem with which Math was regarded, stating in his letter, dated October 29, 1918:

His sterling character, his studiousness and earnestness naturally drew attention from his superior officers….His Colonel trusted him implicitly….(Math) died on the field of battle, Gloriously, my dear Mrs. English….We buried him with military honors and many a manly eye filled with tears as they thought of his beautiful qualities and how they loved him.[47]

On March 28, 1919, the President of the United States, Woodrow Wilson, authorized Math L. English to receive two Distinguished Service Cross awards—the first medal for his

September 26 action at Cheppy which Colonel Patton observed, and the second in the form of an Oak Leaf Cluster to be worn with the Cross for his action October 4 at Exermont during which he was killed.

In the years which followed, a granite monument was erected in Coupeville, near the Island County courthouse, honoring the eight Whidbey Island men who gave their lives in World War I.

Howard English, Math's son, with the Island County memorial in front of the "Lovejoy" County Courthouse in Coupeville. *Math English personal artifacts: Fort Casey Collection.*

Approximately fourteen years later, Math's wife, having remarried and moved to Victoria, British Columbia, received a letter dated December 13, 1932 from Major Douglass T. Greene of the 66th Infantry (Light Tanks) telling her that a street on Fort George G. Meade in Maryland had been named *English Avenue* in Math's honor and enclosed a photo of the marker.[48]

Photo credit: Math English personal artifacts: Fort Casey Collection.

Epilogue

Captain Math L. English and over five million other Allied soldiers gave their lives "to make the world safe for democracy," hoping that their war would be "the war to end all wars." But it would not be so. Two decades later, a disgruntled World War I German corporal, Adolf Hitler, would rise to power in Munich and embroil Europe in another blood bath. George S. Patton, Jr., promoted to Lieutenant General, would use the lessons from that 1st Tank Corps in 1918 to achieve victories in Sicily and in Belgium. Ironically, he would die from injuries incurred in an automobile accident during the Occupation of Germany following World War II.

Although some disdained his overbearing, do-it-my-way attitude, in the eyes of many "Old Blood-and-Guts" Patton was a hero. Americans lauded his tactical skills during the Battle of the Bulge and mourned his untimely passing. Few but family and close friends would even recall Captain English of Company C, 344th Battalion, 1st Brigade, Tank Corps, A.E.F. 1918.

However, Patton's superior officer during World War I, Brigadier General Samuel D. Rockenbach, recalled a short poem in his possession that Patton had composed while recuperating alone in his hotel room on November 11, 1918 expressing the manner in which he wished to die. Rockenbach released that poem to the

71

Associated Press, and two days after Patton's death, this tribute to
Captain English appeared in America's newspapers.[49]

The war is over and we pass
To pleasure after pain,
Except those few who ne'er shall see
Their native land again.

To one of these my memory turns,
Noblest of the slain;
To Captain English of the tanks
Who never shall return.

Yet should some future war exact
Of me the final debt,
My fondest wish would be to tread
The path which he has set.

For faithful unto God and man
And to his duty true,
He died to live forever
In the hearts of those he knew.

Death found in him no faltering
But, faithful to the last,
He smiled in the face of fate
And mocked him as he passed.

No, death to him was not defeat
But victory sublime;
The grave promoted him to be
A hero for all time.

It is not uncommon for soldiers to write poetry about their war experiences when the possibility of death intensifies emotions. According to his daughter Ruth Ellen Totten, Patton wrote numerous poems near the battlefield "to cheer and inspire himself" for "he was always worried…that he would not be able to face the song of the bullet that had his name on it." [50]

Patton summed up the virtues that he most admired in Captain English with the phrases "faithful unto God and man/ And to his duty true." That concept of patriotic *duty* appears also in Francis Scott Key's final verse of what is now our national anthem: "Then conquer we must/ When our cause, it is just,/ And this be our motto, /In God is our Trust."

Writing the poem *In Flanders Field* at the Battle of Ypres, Belgium in 1915, the Canadian Lieutenant Colonel John McCrae addressed a soldier's duty with the lines "Take up our quarrel with the foe!/ To you from failing hands we throw/The torch, be yours to hold it high!" Katharine Lee Bates amended the third verse of her poem *America the Beautiful* in 1913 to read "O beautiful for heroes proved in liberating strife/Who more than self their country loved/ and mercy more than life!"

Early 20th century Americans believed heroism and patriotism walked hand in hand with the Judeo-Christian principles on which America was founded. The belief that "all men are endowed by their Creator with certain inalienable rights" meant that Americans had a duty to defend those rights, not just for themselves, but for all mankind. Errors in America's war policies may appear in retrospect, but from the Revolutionary shot fired at Lexington Bridge to the War On Terror in Afghanistan, her motive has always been defending the attacked and the oppressed:

—against tyrants from England's George III to Hitler, Mussolini, and Saddam Hussein;

—against enslavement by Muslim pirates along the shores of Tripoli to human trafficking in Africa, Asia, and the Middle East;

—against evil ideologies of fascism, Nazism, communism, and radical Islam.

America has, for the most part, delayed her entrance into the fray until even conscientious objectors like Alvin York, who fought within miles of Captain English in the Argonne campaign, realize that at some point peace-loving people must stand up to the aggressors, the bullies of the world, and say "No more!"

It is worth noting that on April 3, 1918, while Patton, English, and others in Pershing's American Expeditionary Forces gathered in Europe to train for battle, the United States House of Representatives adopted an "American's Creed," written by William Tyler Page which states:

I believe in the United States of America as a government
of the people, by the people, for the people; whose just

powers are derived from the consent of the governed, a
democracy in a republic, a sovereign Nation of many
sovereign States; a perfect union, one and inseparable;
established upon those principles of freedom, equality,
justice, and humanity for which American patriots
sacrificed their lives and fortunes.

I therefore believe it is my duty to my country
to love it, to support its Constitution, to obey its laws,
to respect its flag, and to defend it against all enemies.

George Patton admired, even coveted, that faithfulness to duty which he saw demonstrated by Captain Math L. English. Yet, someone may wonder while walking among the thousands of graves in American war cemeteries around the world—from Omaha Beach to Pearl Harbor, Arlington to Manila, Luxembourg where Patton is buried, and the Meuse-Argonne where English lies with 14,000 comrades—what sets Captain English apart from these? Primarily his story can be told because someone observed his actions and lived to report them. He exemplifies the American soldier, not seeking aggression for thrills and glory, but willing to give his all protecting liberty, his family, and the homeland that he loves. The first fifteen years of Math's military career were spent *defending* America, "never firing a gun in anger" at Fort Casey. Fighting was not his primary objective. Most likely, had he lived to receive his medal, he would have answered as so many decorated American soldiers have, "I only did my duty."

May the story of Captain English of the Tanks represent the thousands of Americans who have likewise answered duty's call, and may it inspire future generations to defend American ideals and principles, "faithful to the last" as they "tread the path which he has set...A hero for all time."

Notes

[1] Robert H. Patton, *The Pattons: A Personal History of an American Family.* (New York: Crown Publishers, Inc., 1994), 185.

[2] www.findagrave,com, Glascock County, Georgia, English Family Cemetery, Joel Isaac English.

[3] www.findagrave.com, Glascock County, Georgia, Gibson City Cemetery, William Rooks Logue.

[4] David M. Hansen, *Battle Ready. The National Coast Defense System and the Fortification of Puget Sound, 1894-1925.* (Pullman, WA: Washington State University Press, 2014), 7-12.

[5] Ibid., 111.

[6] General Orders No. 80, Headquarters, Department of the Columbia Vancouver Barracks, Washington, July 23, 1910.

[7] Fred Terrell, as told to the author, Summer, 2006.

[8] Mimi Sheridan, AICP. *How Coupeville Grew.* (McConnell/Burke, Inc., June 1998), 14.

[9] Mary Kline Rose, *A Great Blessing: The First 150 Years of the Coupeville United Methodist Church.* (Vancouver, Washington: Rose Wind Press, 2003), 111 and 142.

[10] Ibid., 111.

[11] *Captain Math L. English Historical Collection, Fort Casey State Park,* 2nd ed. (Fort Casey, WA: July 2004).

[12] Roger M. Sherman, *The Sinking of the Calista Part One: A Maritime History of Central Whidbey Island.* (1998).

[13] *Island County Times,* (Coupeville, WA, December 22, 1916), 1.

[14] *Island County Times,* May 28, 1915, 1.

[15] *Island County Times,* April 13, 1917, 1.

[16] *Fort Casey Historical Collection,* Captain Edmund Hébert letter, October 29, 1918.

[17] Ibid. French postcard.

[18] *Island County Times,* (Island County Historical Society Museum archives, no date).

[19] *Island County Times,* November 9, 1917.

[20] Dale E. Wilson, *Treat 'Em Rough: The Birth of American Armor, 1917-20.* (Novato, CA: Presidio Press, 1990), 13.

[21] Wilson, *Treat 'Em Rough,* 35.

[22] *Island County Times,* December 6, 1918.

[23] *Island County Times,* no date, (Island County Historical Society Museum archives.)

[24] Unless otherwise noted, all battle details regarding locations, movements, times, numbers of tanks are from Wilson, *Treat 'Em Rough,* 89-114.

[25] Wilson, *Treat 'Em Rough,* 101.

[26] Patton, *The Pattons,* 179-180.

[27] Battle details again from Wilson, *Treat 'Em Rough,* 119-151.

[28] Harvey L. Harris, *The War As I Saw It: 1918 Letters of a Tank Corps Lieutenant.* (St. Paul, Minnesota: Pogo Press Inc. 1998), 90.

[29] Patton, *The Pattons,* 182-183.

[30] *Fort Casey Historical Collection,* Distinguished Service Cross certificate.

[31] Patton, *The Pattons, 183.*

[32] Ibid.

[33] Ibid.

[34] Ibid., 185-186.

[35] Battle details from Wilson, *Treat 'Em Rough,* 156-158.

[36] Harris, *The War As I Saw It,* 96.

[37] Ibid., 130.

[38] Ibid.

[39] Ibid., 132.

[40] Wilson, *Treat 'Em Rough,* 158.

[41] General Orders No. 37, W.D., 1919.

[42] *Fort Casey Historical Collection,* Dr. E. F. Ristine letter.

[43] *Fort Casey Historical Collection.*

[44] Ibid.

[45] Ibid.

[46] Ibid.

[47] Ibid.

[48] Ibid.

[49] Associated Press release. *Patton Poem Is Revealed.* Brownsville, Tex. December 26, 1945.

[50] Ruth Ellen Patton Totten, *The Button Box: A Daughter's Loving Memoir of Mrs. George S. Patton.* (Columbia, MO, University of Missouri Press, 2011), 117.

Appendix A

$-45-$

Certificate of Marriage.

STATE OF WASHINGTON, } ss.
COUNTY OF ISLAND.

I HEREBY CERTIFY, That on the _sixteenth_ day of _March_ in the year of our Lord one thousand nine hundred and _ten_, at _Coupeville_ in the County of _Island_ and State aforesaid, I, the undersigned, a _Minister of the Gospel_ by authority of a license bearing date the _14th_ day of _March_ A. D. 19_1_0, and issued by the County Auditor of _Island_ County, did, on the _16th_ day of _March_ A. D. 1910, join in lawful wedlock _Mathew L English_ of the County of _Island_ State of _Wash_ and _Mary A Howard_ of the County of _Island_ State of _Washington_

In Presence of

Bessie Crowell }
James Howard } Witnesses.

Mathew L English Groom.

E. S. Ireland
Minister of the Gospel

Mary A Howard Bride.

Filed for Record this _18th_ day of _March_ A. D. 19_1_0

By _____

J. C. Power
Clerk

This Certificate must be filled out and filed with the County Clerk of the County WHERE THE CEREMONY IS PERFORMED, within three months after the ceremony.—See Hill's Code, Vol. 1, Sec. 1386.

The County Clerk's fee for recording this certificate is One Dollar, to be paid by the party applying for the license at the time each license is issued.—Hill's Code, Vol. 1, Sec. 1387.

Failure to make and deliver Certificate to the County Clerk within three months is punishable by a fine of not less than $25.00 or more than $300.00.

VAN OLINDA, PRINTER, COUPEVILLE, WASH.

a

Appendix B

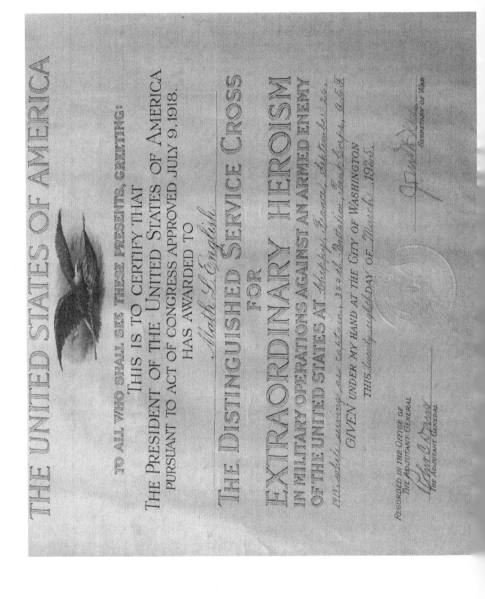

Appendix C

Army of the United States of America

To all who shall see these presents, greeting:

This is to certify that

Nath L. English,

Captain, Tank Corps,

died with honor in the service of this country
on the _____ Fourth _____ day of _____ October _____, 19 18

Given at Washington, D.C., office of The Adjutant General of the Army,
this _____ Third _____ day of _____ January _____, one thousand nine hundred and twenty.

Adjutant General.

Form No. 667 A.G.O.
June 2, 1920

C

d

Bibliography

Associated Press release. *Patton Poem Is Revealed.* Brownsville, Texas, December 26, 1945.

Bausum, Ann. *Sergeant Stubby: How a Stray Dog and His Best Friend Helped Win World War I and Stole the Heart of a Nation.* Washington D.C.: National Geographic Society, 2014.

Berhow, Mark A. *American Seacoast Defenses: A Reference Guide,* Third Edition. McLean, Virginia: Coast Defense Study Group Press, 2015.

Blumenson, Martin. *Patton: The Man Behind the Legend, 1885-1945.* New York: Quill, William Morrow and Company, Inc., 1985.

Captain Math L. English Historical Collection, Fort Casey State Park, 2nd edition. Fort Casey, WA: July 2004.

Clark, Mickey. *Ebey's Landing National Historical Reserve Oral History Project: Fort Casey and Related Subjects.* Tape 95.1.18, December 4, 1995.

Crocker, H.W. III. *The Yanks Are Coming! A Military History of the United States in World War I.* New York: Regnery History, 2014.

Eisenhower, John S. D. *Yanks: The Epic Story of the American Army in World War I.* New York: The Free Press, 2001.

Hansen, David M. *Battle Ready. The National Coast Defense System and the Fortification of Puget Sound, 1894-1925.* Pullman, WA: Washington State University Press, 2014.

e

Harris, Harvey L. *The War As I Saw It: 1918 Letters of a Tank Corps Lieutenant.* St. Paul, Minnesota: Pogo Press, Inc., 1998.

How Coupeville Grew: A Short History of Town Development— Excerpts from the Town of Coupeville's Historic Preservation Plan. A Joint Project of the Town of Coupeville, Trust Board of Ebey's Landing National Historical Reserve, and National Park Service, 1998.

Island County Times. Edited and owned by W. T. Howard, Coupeville, WA, 1909 to 1918. Oak Harbor, WA: Sno-Isle Library archives.

Mitchell, F. M. C. *Tank Warfare: The Story of the Tanks in the Great War.* London: Thomas Nelson and Sons. Ltd., 1933.

Captain Matthew L. English, Killed in Action, Oct. 4th, 1918. Seattle: *The Niles News,* February, 1919.

Patton, Robert H. *The Pattons: A Personal History of an American Family.* New York: Crown Publishers, Inc., 1994.

Rose, Mary Kline. *A Great Blessing: The First 150 Years of the Coupeville United Methodist Church.* Vancouver, Washington: Rose Wind Press, 2003.

Sherman, Roger M. *The Sinking of the Calista Part One: A Maritime History of Central Whidbey Island.* 1998.

Totten, Ruth Ellen Patton. *The Button Box: A Daughter's Loving Memoir of Mrs. George S. Patton.* Columbia, Missouri: University of Missouri Press, 2011.

Wilson, Dale E. *Treat 'Em Rough: The Birth of American Armor, 1917-20.* Novato, CA: Presidio Press, 1990.

f

Alternative sources

www.findagrave.com, Glascock County, Georgia, English Family Cemetery, Joel Isaac English

www.findagrave.com, Glascock County, Georgia, Gibson City Cemetery, William Rooks Logue

Janet Enzmann Library and Archives, Island County Historical Society Museum, Coupeville, WA.

Swint, Matt. Glascock County Consolidated School, Gibson, Georgia, personal email Aug 14, 2015.

Wikipedia. *America the Beautiful* - Lyrics.

h

About the Author

Anita Burdette-Dragoo is retired following a twenty-year career with the Department of Defense, teaching military dependent children on U.S. bases overseas. While assigned to Germany, she spent several hours in the same ER at Heidelberg Army Hospital, according to a bronze plaque on the Emergency Room wall, where Patton was treated following the accident that resulted in his death.

Members of Burdette-Dragoo's family have served in every war of the 20th century including the Cold War, a total of 20 veterans in the Army, Navy, Marines, or Air Force, from the great-uncle who wrote poetry in France during World War I, as did Patton, until he died in a hospital in Nevers after being gassed on the battlefield to the cousin who entered Iraq with the tanks during Desert Storm.

Today she lives with her husband, a retired submariner and Seabee, near Fort Casey where Math English once served on Whidbey Island, Washington.

j

INDEX

I

m

Made in the USA
Charleston, SC
19 August 2016